To every child   A.M.

Text by Mary Joslin
Illustrations copyright © 2013 Alida Massari
This edition copyright © 2013 Lion Hudson

Published by Lion Children's Books
an imprint of
Lion Hudson plc
Wilkinson House, Jordan Hill Road,
Oxford OX2 8DR, England
www.lionhudson.com/lionchildrens

ISBN 978 0 7459 6116 3

First edition 2013

A catalogue record for this book is available from the British Library

Printed and bound in China, July 2013, LH17

The Story of Christmas

DUDLEY PUBLIC LIBRARIES

The loan of this book may be renewed if not required by other readers, by contacting the library from which it was borrowed.

The Story of Christmas

This is how it happened...

Mary Joslin ILLUSTRATED BY Alida Massari

LION
CHILDREN'S

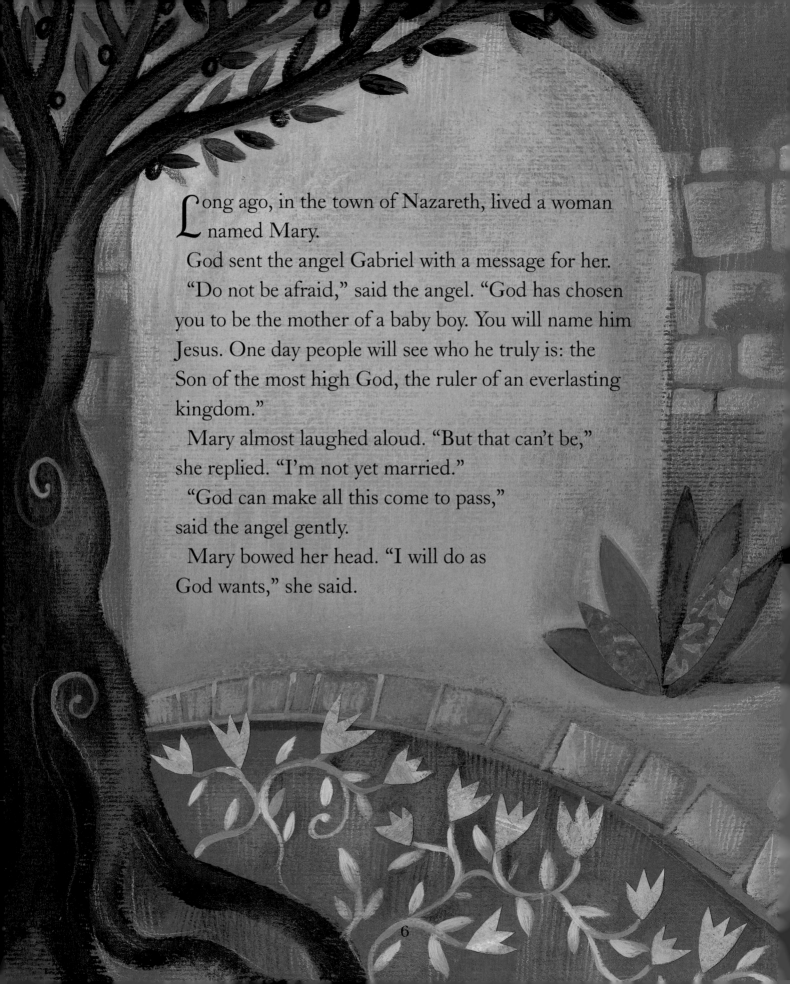

Long ago, in the town of Nazareth, lived a woman named Mary.

God sent the angel Gabriel with a message for her.

"Do not be afraid," said the angel. "God has chosen you to be the mother of a baby boy. You will name him Jesus. One day people will see who he truly is: the Son of the most high God, the ruler of an everlasting kingdom."

Mary almost laughed aloud. "But that can't be," she replied. "I'm not yet married."

"God can make all this come to pass," said the angel gently.

Mary bowed her head. "I will do as God wants," she said.

Joseph was the carpenter in Nazareth. When he heard that Mary was expecting a baby, he thought he would never be happy again.

"It was all arranged for Mary and me to marry," he said to himself. "But her baby isn't my baby.

"The wedding can't go ahead now."

Then in a quiet voice an angel spoke. "Don't be afraid, Joseph, and don't be sad.

"God still wants you to marry Mary, and to take care of her and her baby."

Joseph saw at once what he must do. He went to tell Mary.

"The emperor who rules this land has demanded that everyone register as taxpayers," he said.

"I will have to go to Bethlehem to do that. My family is descended from the great King David of long ago. Bethlehem was his home town and is also mine.

"We will go there together, and register as husband and wife."

And so they made the long journey.

Many others were making the same journey for the same reason. When Mary and Joseph reached Bethlehem, all the rooms for visitors were full.

They had to shelter in a stable, where the donkey stamped and shuffled and a patient ox munched its hay.

There, in the night, Mary's baby was born. She wrapped him in swaddling clothes and cradled him in a manger.

Out on the hillside, shepherds were watching their sheep.

"It's hard having to stay up on a cold, dark night," grumbled one. "And who knows what dangers we'll face. Hush… was that a wolf I heard? I'd rather it were a wolf than a bear."

"I don't mind the dark of night as much as I mind the dark times we live in," said another. "That tyrant Herod in Jerusalem, and a foreign emperor in Rome, greedy to claim our money in taxes."

"What we need is a messiah," said a third. "A king like great King David of old. Someone to set us free."

Suddenly the night sky turned to gold.
An angel cried out in a joyful shout.
"I bring good news – to you and all the world!
"A child has been born in Bethlehem. Tonight he is cradled in a manger.
"One day everyone will see that he is God's chosen king, the messiah, the Christ."
And with that, a thousand thousand angels began to sing.

Glory to God!
Peace on earth.

Then the angels were gone.
"Was I dreaming?" asked one of the shepherds.
"Were we all dreaming?" asked another. "Come on!
Let's go and find out."

There in the stable they found Mary and Joseph and the baby, just as the angel had said.

From far away to the east, wise men came riding.
They were following a new star that had
appeared in the night sky, believing it would
lead them to a newborn king.

It led them first to Jerusalem, where King Herod summoned them to his palace.

Any new king was a rival, and he would not tolerate that.

"The learned men in my court can help you," he told the foreigners. "The ancient books of our people say that one day the greatest king of all will be born in Bethlehem.

"Try to find your star-heralded king there.

"Then come and tell everything to me."

As the wise men left Jerusalem, the star lit their way.
It shone over a humble room in Bethlehem.
There they found Jesus with his mother, Mary.
They offered gifts in tribute: gold, frankincense,
and myrrh.

They did not go back to Herod in Jerusalem.
Angels showed them another way to their homeland.
And angels also whispered to Joseph:
"Herod knows about Jesus and plans to harm him.
"Hurry: take Mary and her child to safety."
For Jesus was God's Son, born to bring God's
blessing to all the world.

Other titles from Lion Children's Books

The Animals' Christmas *Elena Pasquali & Giuliano Ferri*

The First Christmas *Lois Rock & Sophie Allsopp*

The Lion Storyteller Christmas Book *Bob Hartman & Krisztina Kállai Nagy*

Women of the Bible *Margaret McAllister & Alida Massari*